PRAYER
YOUR
FOUNDATION
FOR
SUCCESS
WORKBOOK

KENNETH
COPELAND

KENNETH COPELAND
PUBLICATIONS

Prayer—Your Foundation for Success Workbook

ISBN 978-1-57562-627-7   30-0076

22 21 20 19 18 17   7 6 5 4 3 2

© 1983, 2013 Kenneth Copeland

Kenneth Copeland Publications
Fort Worth, TX 76192-0001

For more information about Kenneth Copeland Ministries, call 1-800-600-7395 (U.S. only) or +1-817-852-6000, or visit www.kcm.org.

Table of Contents

Introduction
A Message From Kenneth Copeland

*As a believer, you can achieve the same
results that Jesus did during His earthly
ministry—and more.*

"Verily, verily, I say unto you, He that believeth on
me, the works that I do shall he do also; and greater
works than these shall he do; because I go
unto my Father."

John 14:12

1. What is the key to success in every area of life?

Prayer and fellowship with the Father

2. What did Jesus do that prepared Him to minister effectively?

Spend much time in prayer and fellowship with His Father

3. Is it realistic to expect to achieve the same results Jesus did during His earthly ministry? If so, how? If not, why not?

He said it was - I have not obtained that maybe because of a lack of deep prayer + fellowship with my Father

CHAPTER ONE
Prayer Secrets

Prayer is the foundation of every successful Christian endeavor.

"Men ought always to pray, and not to faint."

Luke 18:1

1. Brother Copeland compares the Body of Christ to a brick building. Mortar is used to hold the bricks together. What knits the Body of Christ together?

The power of love through prayer and intercession

2. What should happen if a member of the Body of Christ is injured or weakened?

The others should stand in prayer and make up for that weakness.

> { *The very heart of a successful prayer life is deep and intimate fellowship with the Father.* }

3. What pleases God and causes your prayers to bring results?

Deep intimate fellowship with Him.

4. How does God manifest Himself in the earth?

Through the believer who operates in faith

5. What is the "mother" of faith?

Fellowship is the' mother of faith.

6. What does your new birth give you the right to expect?

The right to expect your prayers to be answered

7. What is the No. 1 priority in God's heart?

To spend quality time with us daily.

8. What does it mean to "bear fruit" as stated in John 15:7-8?

Bearing fruit is doing the works of Jesus therefore pleasing the Father

> { *Set aside time every day to spend with your heavenly Father.* }

9. What is the way to bear fruit?

Fruit bearing comes through prayer

10. How did Jesus stay in tune with the Holy Spirit?

He spent time in prayer and fellowship with the Father

11. What happens when you pray in faith and confidence?

All of heaven's resources are at your disposal.

Discussion Question

Which "prayer secrets" that were expressed in this chapter will you apply to your life and ministry?

_____

_____

_____

_____

_____

_____

_____

_____

_____

_____

_____

_____

_____

_____

_____

_____

_____

_____

_____

_____

_____

CHAPTER TWO
Praying for Results

God's Word is His will. When you have prayed in line with the Word, you have automatically prayed in line with God's will.

"What things soever ye desire, when ye pray, believe that ye receive them, and ye shall have them."

Mark 11:24

1. What is the major cause of failure in Christian enterprises?

Lack of prayer

_____

_____

_____

2. Brother Copeland tells us that it is possible to spend all your time in prayer. How can this be accomplished?

_____

_____

_____

_____

_____

_____

3. How do you get results in prayer?

_____

_____

_____

_____

_____

{ *Prayer is communicating with God.* }

4. What is prayer?

_____

_____

_____

_____

5. What is the key to success in prayer?

_____

_____

_____

_____

6. What is the No. 1 rule in praying for results?

_____

_____

_____

{ *The key to success in prayer is expecting results.* }

7. How can we know the will of God for our lives?

_____

_____

_____

_____

8. What places a qualification on your prayer?

_____

_____

_____

_____

9. Where does faith come from, and how do you get it?

_____

_____

_____

_____

_____

10. How did Jesus release power in His earthly ministry? Explain.

_____

_____

_____

_____

_____

11. What puts faith into motion?

_____

_____

_____

{ *Faith is released with the mouth. Words are the vehicles.* }

12. How was Peter able to walk on the water?

_____

_____

_____

_____

13. How do you refuse doubt, fear and unbelief?

_____

_____

_____

_____

_____

_____

_____

_____

_____

_____

_____

_____

_____

_____

_____

_____

_____

14. How can you avoid failure?

_____

15. When you pray in Jesus' Name according to the Word of God, in faith, what will happen?

_____

_____

_____

_____

_____

{ *Prepare to succeed!* }

Discussion Question

How should we pray to get results?

_____

_____

_____

_____

_____

_____

_____

_____

CHAPTER THREE
The Battlefield of Prayer

The armor described in Ephesians 6 is prayer armor. It serves one vital purpose: to combat Satan and win!

"Finally, my brethren, be strong in the Lord, and in the power of his might. Put on the whole armour of God, that ye may be able to stand against the wiles of the devil...that ye may be able to withstand in the evil day, and having done all, to stand."

Ephesians 6:10-11, 13

1. What are the weapons of our warfare, and what is our responsibility in using them?

_____

_____

_____

_____

_____

2. How does Satan overtake us?

_____

_____

_____

_____

_____

> { *Your enemy is not other people. Satan is the source of your trouble.* }

3. What are the components of our armor?

_____

_____

_____

_____

_____

4. What should be our strategy when Satan tells us we won't see the manifestation of our prayers?

_____

_____

_____

_____

_____

5. How is faith compared to planting a seed?

_____

_____

_____

_____

_____

{ *Your faith makes you an overcomer and more than a conqueror!* }

6. Why do we use the Name of Jesus in spiritual warfare?

_____

_____

_____

_____

_____

7. What is the power behind the Name of Jesus?

_____

_____

_____

_____

8. The _____ of your prayer life depends on the degree of _____ you place in the _____ _____.

9. He is your _____, sent to bear you up.... The operation of the Holy Spirit should be a _____ to you.

10. When you know _why_ you have _____ over Satan, you will be _____ to use that _____.

11. God gave man His _____ and_____.

12. What did God have to do to redeem mankind?

_____

_____

_____

_____

13. Jesus had to die both _____ and _____.

{ *Keep your thoughts on the Word. It is the answer to your problems.* }

14. How did Jesus fulfill the Abrahamic covenant?

_____

_____

_____

_____

15. Jesus identified with the _____ _____ and became our _____ _____. He paid an awesome _____ for our _____.

16. When a believer speaks the Word of God with authority, you can't tell the difference between him and _____.

Discussion Question

What weapons of our warfare should we use to fight the good fight of faith on the battlefield of prayer?

_____

_____

_____

_____

_____

_____

_____

_____

_____

_____

_____

CHAPTER FOUR
Prayer That Changes Things

———◆———

Always remember that prayer changes things—not God.

"Verily I say unto you, Whatsoever ye shall bind on earth shall be bound in heaven: and whatsoever ye shall loose on earth shall be loosed in heaven. Again I say unto you, That if two of you shall agree on earth as touching any thing that they shall ask, it shall be done for them of my Father which is in heaven. For where two or three are gathered together in my name, there am I in the midst of them."

Matthew 18:18-20

1. What are the types of prayer that can be used to change things?

a._____

b._____

c._____

d._____

e._____

f. _____

2. Prayer changes _____. It doesn't change _____.

3. One of the mighty attributes of God is _____ _____.

4. What you want to do is take your _____ and _____ _____ _____ _____ and change the _____ in your life to line up with His will.

5. His plans and desires are always for your _____ and _____-_____.

6. The Word says that God's eyes are over the righteous, and His ears are open to _____ _____ (Psalm _____).

{ *The prayer of agreement will cover every circumstance of life.* }

7. The prayer of agreement will cover _____
_____ __ _____. Its foundation scripture is found in
_____ which states:

_____

_____

_____

_____

_____

8. How did Brother Copeland and Gloria use the prayer of
agreement regarding their finances?

_____

_____

_____

_____

_____

_____

_____

9. Jesus said that if any _____ on earth agree, He
would be in the midst of that _____ to see that it
comes to pass.

10. What did Jesus say in Mark 11:25-26 that you should do
when you pray?

_____

_____

_____

_____

11. In Galatians 5:6, the Bible says that faith works by
_____. If you are operating with an _____ _____,
your prayer life will be_____.

12. _____makes prayer work.

13. Build your _____, your _____, and _____
_____ _____ of your life on the _____
love of God.

14. When you _____ and reach for
_____, you come to a place where you have the
_____ _____ to perceive the _____ of
_____.

15. When you are in _____ and _____
with those around you, you will step into a _____,
more _____ _____ with _____.

16. God intends for the Body of Christ to _____
the evil forces of this world.

17. The prayer of _____ and _____
halts Satan's activities.

{ *We are to spoil Satan's plans, plots and maneuvers against God's people!* }

18. As you enforce the _____ vested in the
_____, speak directly to _____. Exercise
your faith in the work of Jesus at Calvary.

19. The _____ _____ is yours whether
or not to _____ from God.

20. The words _____ and _____
are defined as "a formal _____ addressed to a
_____ _____."

21. An absolutely tremendous amount of _____
is involved in _____ _____.

22. As a _____ of _____, we need to get
in _____ _____ on the _____
of _____ and _____ results.

Discussion Question

In your current situation, which type of prayer discussed in
this chapter would be most appropriate? Why?

_____

_____

_____

_____

_____

_____

_____

_____

_____

_____

_____

CHAPTER FIVE

Intercessory Prayer

Through His Word, God has called the Body of Christ to the ministry of intercession.

"I exhort therefore, that, first of all, supplications, prayers, intercessions, and giving of thanks, be made for all men; for kings, and for all that are in authority; that we may lead a quiet and peaceable life in all godliness and honesty. For this is good and acceptable in the sight of God our Saviour; who will have all men to be saved, and to come unto the knowledge of the truth."

1 Timothy 2:1-4

1. The prayer of _____ is prayed in _____ of _____.

2. We are to call on Him to pour out of _____ _____ in these last days in great, unusual _____ of His _____.

3. We are the most _____ generation to have ever lived on this earth. We are _____ not only to _____ these manifestations, but also to be the _____ through which His mighty _____ will flow.

> { *Intercessory prayer is the tool that the Spirit of God uses to bring miracles into manifestation.* }

4. Why are we called to intercession?

_____

_____

_____

_____

5. Brother Copeland believes that we are the generation that will _____ in the _____ of the Lord Jesus Christ for His _____.

6. When you are born again, you do not become a
_____ of _____. You become a
_____ of _____. In order to become
a _____ or _____, you must make a
_____.

7. Because of your love for God, _____ choose
to _____ Him. You yield your _____ to
His will and become a _____-_____ with Him.

8. Paul had the right to go free. He served His Master out of
_____ and _____.

9. Prayer is the _____ into the mightiest release
of _____ that is known to man.

10. _____ is the highest expression of love.

11. _____has _____ the _____of those
who have not received the gospel. Your _____ _____
wrestles against _____ _____that have deceived them.

{ *When you respond to the call of intercession, the Holy Spirit prays the perfect will of God through you.* }

12. What motivated God to send Jesus?

_____

_____

13. Jesus has provided _____between God and man through His _____ sacrifice at Calvary. We are _____-_____ with Him.

14. God yearns for every sinner to be _____ to Himself through the _____ _____, and every believer to be in close_____ with Him.

15. To give your life [to Jesus] means to give _____.

16. Through the _____ of God's Word, we realize His _____ is in us. That _____ urges us to reach out to _____. It urges us to be _____ _____.

{ *Intercession gives the Holy Spirit the opportunity to bring the fullness of God's will to pass in the earth.* }

17. Praying in _____ _____ is the most _____ tool that you have in _____ prayer.

18. _____ _____ from the things of this _____. Get in your prayer closet _____ ____ ____ and commit to intercession.

19. _____ is God's heartbeat because it is the labor that births the souls of this world into His family.

20. God's purpose is for us to begin to pray for _____.

Discussion Question

Brother Copeland stated that intercession is the highest expression of love. With this in mind, what can you do to express this kind of love toward a family member or friend today?

_____

_____

_____

_____

_____

_____

_____

_____

_____

_____

_____

_____

_____

_____

_____

_____

CHAPTER SIX
Kinds of Prayer

There is more than just one kind of prayer,
depending on what you desire from the Lord.

"Stand therefore...praying always with all
prayer and supplication in the Spirit, and
watching thereunto with all perseverance
and supplication for all saints."

Ephesians 6:14, 18

1. God's Word instructs us to "pray always with _____ _____."

2. The prayer of dedication and worship holds a tremendous amount of _____.

3. The only time the word _____ would *not* be an expression of _____ is in the prayer of dedication and worship.

4. _____ hinders prayer.

5. The prayer of dedication is getting your _____ in line with God's _____ to bring _____ into the situation.

6. When you pray the prayer of dedication and live by it, you will experience the _____ of God because you are truly _____ _____ _____.

7. Faith involves _____ and _____.

8. You and God are working _____. It is your _____ and His _____.

9. Praise is more than just _____. There is _____ in it.

{ *You cannot face any problem that has not been taken care of through Calvary's cross.* }

10. The only way _____ can stop you and your _____ is through _____. He does not have the _____ to stop _____.

11. Praise is not something you just _____ once in a while. God is _____ of your _____. The Bible says to offer the _____ of praise.

12. As a new-covenant believer, you are a _____ of God. No other sacrifice can be offered. Jesus offered the ultimate _____ _____. As a priest, you offer the sacrifice of _____.

13. God is vehemently against _____. It does not produce anything but _____, _____ and _____.

{ *The Greater One dwells in you. He is able to put you over!* }

14. We must cast our _____ over on the Lord and not take them back.

15. God's _____ comes by acting on His _____ that says to cast _____ of your _____ and _____ over on Him. You must _____ those thoughts with _____ _____.

16. The power of God begins to _____ when you _____ your care over on Him.

Discussion Question

Considering what you are seeking the Lord for at this very moment, which kind of prayer mentioned in this chapter is most appropriate to address your need?

_____

_____

_____

_____

_____

_____

_____

_____

_____

_____

_____

_____

_____

_____

_____

_____

_____

_____

CHAPTER SEVEN
Fasting and Prayer

Fasting changes you, *not God!*

"Moreover when ye fast, be not, as the hypocrites, of a sad countenance: for they disfigure their faces, that they may appear unto men to fast. Verily I say unto you, they have their reward. But thou, when thou fastest, anoint thine head, and wash thy face; that thou appear not unto men to fast, but unto thy Father which is in secret: and thy Father, which seeth in secret, shall reward thee openly."

Matthew 6:16-18

1. There are two categories of fasting: a _____ fast (Joel 1:14), and a _____ fast as Jesus described in Matthew 6.

2. You do not fast to _____ God. Some people think that if they _____ long enough, it will _____ Him to do something for them. Punishing yourself does not _____ the Lord. It will only make you very, very _____! Fasting changes _____, not God.

3. Sometimes _____ arise in which you need _____ _____. A _____ fast brings _____ into a place of _____ _____ _____.

4. The main reason a _____ fast brings results is because it directs people's _____ toward God.

5. What did Jesus say about the personal fast in Matthew 6:16-18?

_____

_____

_____

_____

_____

{ *An open reward comes from God when you fast in secret.* }

6. Rewards for personal fasting are on two different levels. One is from the _____ of _____.

7. There are also personal, _____ rewards.

8. God told Joshua to _____ on the _____ day and night so he would _____ ___ __ all that was _____ in it (Joshua 1:8). In other words, it will be _____ to you how to act on what is _____ in the _____.

9. When the _____ operates in the _____ of God, it prevents _____ from coming in and _____ the effectiveness of the fast. If you are not operating in _____, your fast will not _____ you.

10. Fasting helps you tune in to the _____ _____ where healing—and all your _____— already belongs to you. _____ will shut down the influences of the five physical senses so you can walk in the _____. Your _____, _____, _____, _____ and the _____ of God are all in the _____.

> { *God calls us to fast to bring the spirit man into ascendency over the flesh.* }

11. In Mark 9:28, why did Jesus say the disciples were unable to cast the devil out?

_____

_____

_____

_____

_____

12. Jesus separated Himself to _____ and
_____ regularly. He could _____ to the
people in faith. He stayed _____ _____
His _____ _____—the _____
_____. He lived in _____ to God. A
fasted life, which is _____ and _____,
spending time in the _____, and ministering to
the _____ will keep you in a _____ to
_____ from God.

13. Brother Copeland mentioned that sometimes when
he fasts, the only reward he seeks is the _____ of
a friend, a situation that needs _____, or God's
_____ to minister more effectively. He fasts and
expects the _____ of God to operate.

14. A man living a _____ life lays things aside
just to be with God.

15. What does it mean to live the high life of which Jesus
spoke in Matthew 10:38?

_____

_____

_____

_____

_____

16. What is the five-step checklist for fasting?

1. _____

2. _____

3. _____

4. _____

5. _____

17. Living the _____ life will cause you to produce the _____ of the _____ accord-
ing to Galatians 5:22. This _____ comes forth from
the _____ _____ _____. The
_____ _____ is certainly _____
these things, but He is not in you to _____
_____. He is in you to _____
you how to _____ _____. He is your
_____, your _____, your _____
and _____. He gives you the _____; you
bear the _____.

18. Galatians 5:22-23 says, "But the fruit of the Spirit is
_____, _____, _____,
_____ [patience], _____, _____,
_____, _____, _____: against such
there is no law." These are _____ _____.

19. Fasting shuts down the influence of the _____,
so the _____ man can _____.

Discussion Question

How does fasting affect your prayer life? Has fasting impacted your ability to hear more clearly from God? Have you seen any long-lasting results from fasting and prayer?

_____

_____

_____

_____

_____

_____

_____

_____

_____

_____

_____

_____

_____

_____

_____

_____

_____

_____

_____

CHAPTER EIGHT
Hindrances to Prayer

―――――

God's desire is to answer every prayer.

"And all things, whatsoever ye shall ask in prayer, believing, ye shall receive."

Matthew 21:22

1. God's desire is to _____ every prayer. He has given us His _____ so we can pray according to _____ _____. Unanswered prayer is not the result of God's _____ to use His _____, but because of _____ we allow to _____ us.

2. The _____ says His eyes look _____ and _____ throughout the _____ to show Himself _____ in behalf of those whose _____ are _____ toward Him (2 Chronicles 16:9).

3. Jesus said in Matthew 21:22, "And _____ things, whatsoever ye shall _____ in prayer, _____, ye shall _____." He did not say that a _____ things you pray for would come to pass, or that just a prayer _____ and _____ would be answered. Jesus said, "And _____ things, whatsoever ye shall _____ in prayer, _____." He said _____. Then, "ye shall _____."

> *Fellowship with the Father brings joy to your relationship with Him.*

4. Two of the greatest hindrances to the believer's prayer life are _____ and _____. Though similar, there are differences. Doubt is the _____ of God's greater _____. It keeps a man in a state of

_____ from Him. Some men _____ there is a God or _____ He will perform His _____ in response to their prayers. As a result, they do not respond to _____ _____. This hinders _____ _____ in their behalf. _____ comes from ignorance of _____ _____.

5._____ is when a man knows there is a God, yet does not believe _____ _____. He knows what the _____ says, but he has _____ to believe what he can _____ and _____ instead. This will definitely _____ his prayer life.

> { *Doubt comes from ignorance of God's Word.* }

6. In order to expel _____ and _____, you must make God's Word _____ _____ in every matter, not allowing _____ _____, or what you think about the situation, to be the _____ _____.

7. When you _____, expect things to change. God's Word will not fail.

8. The second great hindrance to prayer is the _____ of _____ of our _____-_____ with God. Most people do not understand what God actually did in Christ Jesus at _____.

Jesus became our _____ so we could become the _____ of God (2 Corinthians 5:21).

9. James 5:16 says, "The effectual fervent prayer of a _____ man availeth much." You may have read that verse of scripture and thought, *You know, if I were just righteous....* Jesus died for you! The _____ He bought for you at Calvary is more than enough to make your prayers effective. Romans 5:17 says _____ is a gift, and Roman 3:22 says it is "unto all...them that believe."

10. God is moved when a man _____ His Word.

11. _____ qualifies you for answered prayer!

12. You have a God-given right to expect God to _____ your prayer. Don't let the devil deceive you into thinking God will not answer. Jesus said that whatsoever you shall ask the Father in His Name, He will give it to you. As long as you can _____, _____, you will not be defeated. If you know your _____-_____ with God, you will not be _____.

{ *Strife and unforgiveness hinder your prayer life.* }

13. Lack of _____ of our _____ to use the Name of Jesus is the third great hindrance to prayer. A great _____ of knowledge of the _____ in Jesus' Name exists in most _____ circles. John 16:23 says, "And in that day ye shall ask Me nothing. Verily,

verily, I say unto you, whatsoever ye shall ask the Father in My Name, He will give it you."

14. What was the example Brother Copeland shared about Gloria using the Name of Jesus?

_____

_____

_____

_____

_____

15. Another hindrance to prayer is found in Mark 11:25-26. It says, "And when ye stand praying, _____, if ye have aught against any: that your Father also which is in heaven may forgive you your trespasses. But if ye do not forgive, neither will your Father which is in Heaven forgive your trespasses." This is _____. Prayer will not work without _____.

16. _____and _____ hinder your prayer life. _____ is merely acting on _____.

17. The absence of _____ is the key to getting rid of _____ and _____.

18. Lack of knowledge of the value of _____ with God will also hinder your prayer life. If you do not know the importance of close, intimate fellowship with God, you will not likely see results in _____. Set apart a specific time to be alone with Him and to divert all your attention toward Him.

19. The Bible says we have been given in our spirit a cry that says, "Abba, Father." Scholars tell us the closest English word we have to *abba* is "_____." Our relationship with Him has all the freedom of *"Daddy,"* and yet the reverence and respect of *"Father."* You can _____ with God on both levels, as your _____ and as your

_____.

20. Fellowshiping with the Father gives Him the opportunity to _____ His Word to you by His _____.... The Word of God brings _____. Fellowship will cause it to become _____. Fellowship will drive out all _____ and _____. It brings you into a _____ relationship with the Father, and _____ casts out _____. Through intimate _____, God will personally reveal His _____ to you.

21. God and His _____ are one. So when you _____ with Him through His Word, He responds to you by His _____. Learn to _____ with God. Do it by _____ and _____ Him to respond.

Discussion Question

Were there any hindrances mentioned in this chapter that you have had to deal with personally? If so, how did (or are) you dealing with those hindrances?

_____

_____

_____

_____

CHAPTER NINE
A Deeper Life in Prayer

When you become accurate in your prayer life, things will happen.

"And in that day ye shall ask me nothing. Verily, verily, I say unto you, Whatsoever ye shall ask the Father in my name, he will give it you. Hitherto have ye asked nothing in my name: ask, and ye shall receive, that your joy may be full. These things have I spoken unto you in proverbs: but the time cometh, when I shall no more speak unto you in proverbs, but I shall show you plainly of the Father. At that day ye shall ask in my name: and I say not unto you, that I will pray the Father for you: For the Father himself loveth you, because ye have loved me, and have believed that I came out from God."

John 16:23-27

1. Scriptural principles of prayer will bring about an accurate
_____ _____. Accuracy produces results.

2. When you are accurate in your prayer life, you are operating out of your _____ _____ rather than just your _____. Your spiritual _____ are open to the _____ of God. Train yourself not to make a _____ without _____ to the Spirit of God. He is the _____. You are the _____.

{ *Train yourself to not make a move without listening to the Spirit of God.* }

3. If you never attempt to be _____ in prayer, you will never be _____ about the results. You'll just be _____ for something to happen.

4. Pray to the _____ in _____ _____. Jesus endorses your prayer. With His _____, you are given _____ access to the throne of God.

{ *With the Name of Jesus, you are given free access to the throne of God.* }

{ *Operate by faith instead of by feeling.* }

5. Believe you receive when you _____.

6. Forgive. Your _____ will not work accurately in an unforgiving _____.

{ *Keep the forgiveness door to your heart open.* }

7. Depend on the _____ _____ in your prayer life.

8. Allow the spirit realm to become a _____ to you. Purpose to see beyond the realm of your five _____ _____. Remember, you are a _____. You have a _____. You live in a _____. Your body is just the _____ _____ for your spirit. It is not the real you.

9. God will confirm His Word to you when you are in _____.

10. Learn to pray for _____.

11. Anytime the Church of Jesus Christ is in _____,

its members are not praying for _____.

12. We are to supply _____ _____ as we draw from God through our fellowship with Him.

13. As you become involved with _____ _____ for the Body of Christ, the whole operation will begin to be successful.

{ *Learn to pray for others.* }

14. Spend time praying in the _____.

15. First Corinthians 14:4 says, "He that speaketh in an _____ _____ edifieth himself." The word *edify* translated in the Greek means the same as "charging a battery."

16. Praying in _____ _____ will keep you tuned in to the _____.

17. God needs a Church that is not walking after the _____. As we walk in the _____ and sow to the _____, we stay "charged" and ready to do battle in the spirit! God needs each one of us in this _____ time.

18. Always base your prayer on the _____ of _____.

Discussion Question

The Apostle Paul declares in Romans 4:19-21 *(New International Version)*, that Abraham "did not waver through unbelief regarding the promise of God, but was strengthened in his faith and gave glory to God, being fully persuaded that God had power to do what he had promised." Are you fully persuaded that God can fulfill His promise to you? Explain.

_____

_____

_____

_____

_____

_____

_____

_____

_____

_____

_____

_____

_____

_____

_____

_____

_____

_____

_____

CHAPTER TEN
Prayers

———————◦◦◦———————

Prayer that is based on the Word is already in line with the will of God.

"And this is the confidence that we have in him, that, if we ask any thing according to his will, he heareth us: And if we know that he hear us, whatsoever we ask, we know that we have the petitions that we desired of him."

1 John 5:14-15

1. The _____ or _____ of the Word by the believer activates the _____ of God.

2. As you speak _____ _____ over situations and _____, it will produce a positive effect and _____ in those areas.

3. Make Jesus the _____ of your life. You are the reason God sent _____ to the cross.

4. God is not holding your _____ against you. He sent Jesus as your _____. He paid the _____. Now you can receive the _____ for what He did in your place (Isaiah 53:3-5).

5. The _____ _____ is the One who endues us with _____ for our Christian walk and to do the _____ of Jesus (John 14:12).

6. Once you are born again, you can receive the _____ _____ just as you received Jesus—by faith in God's Word.

{ *God is alert and active, watching over His Word to perform it.* }

7. A Prayer for Salvation in Behalf of Others:

Father, I come before You in prayer and in _____, _____. Your Word says You desire all _____ to be saved and come into the knowledge of the _____.

8. A Prayer for Health and Healing:

Father, in the Name of Jesus, I confess Your Word concerning healing. I believe and say that Your Word will not return to You _____, but will accomplish what it says it will. Therefore, I believe in the _____ ____ _____, that I am healed according to 1 Peter 2:24. It is written in Your Word that Jesus Himself took my _____ and bore my _____ (Matthew 8:17). Therefore, with great _____ and _____, I say on the _____ of that written Word that I am _____ from the _____ of sickness, and I refuse to _____ its symptoms.

9. A Prayer for Harmonious Marriage:

Father, in the Name of Jesus, it is written in Your Word that _____ is shed abroad in our _____ by the Holy Ghost who is given to us. Because You are in us, we acknowledge that _____ reigns supreme....

Father, we believe and say that we are _____, _____, _____, _____ and _____-_____. We seek _____, and it keeps our hearts in _____ and _____. Because we follow after_____ and dwell in _____, our prayers are not hindered in any way in the Name of Jesus.

10. A Prayer for Your Children:

Father, Your Word is _____, and I believe it. Therefore, in the Name of Jesus, I believe in my _____ and say with my _____ that Your Word

_____ *over my children. Your Word says You will pour out Your Spirit upon my _____, and Your blessing upon my _____.*

11. A Prayer for Our Government:

Father, in Jesus' Name, I give thanks for our country and its _____. I hold up in prayer before You the men and women in positions of _____. I pray for all people in _____ over us in any way. I pray the Spirit of the Lord _____ upon them....

Your Word declares that "blessed is the nation whose God is the Lord." I receive Your _____ and declare with my mouth that Your _____ dwell safely in this land and that they prosper abundantly....

I proclaim that Jesus is _____ over my _____.

{ *God is not holding your sin against you.* }

12. Prayer: To Walk in the Perfect Peace of God:

Father, in Jesus' Name, I thank You that Your peace is my _____ right in Christ Jesus. I will keep my _____ fixed on You, trust in You, and You will keep me in _____ peace.

I will not fret or have _____ about anything, but in every _____ and in everything by prayer and petition

with _____, I will continue to make my wants known
to You, Father....

I will let Your peace rule in my heart.... I will not fear. What
can man do to me? You are my _____ and my
_____. Whom shall I fear or _____? You,
Lord, are the _____ and _____ of my life,
of whom shall I be afraid? I love Your law, O Lord. Nothing shall
offend me or make me stumble. I walk in great_____,
in Jesus' Name. Amen.

13. Prayer: Walking in the Wisdom and Guidance of the
Holy Spirit:

Father, in the Name of Jesus, I realize that, as a believer,
my body is the _____ of the _____
_____. My acknowledgment of Your _____
on a daily basis makes my faith in You effectual. I believe that
You, Heavenly Father, are _____ _____
and _____ _____ by the Holy Spirit through
my spirit, and illuminating my mind.

As I yield to the Holy Spirit, I believe that my _____
are ordered of the Lord. I _____ and _____
myself wholly to His guidance, expecting Him to cause my
thoughts to become agreeable to His will, so my plans will
be established and succeed. I trust in the Lord with all my
_____ and lean not on my own _____. As
I acknowledge Him, He directs me in paths of righteousness....

I meditate in the Word _____ and _____,
not letting it depart from my _____. I test my
inward witness· with the Word, for the _____ and
the _____ agree. I am _____ to act on

the Word, as well as the prompting of my spirit. I am not a _____ *only, but a* _____ *. Therefore, I am* _____ *in all my deeds.*

{ *The Holy Spirit empowers you with God's own power!* }

14. A Prayer for Your Finances:

Heavenly Father, I have chosen Jesus as the Lord of my life, and I seek first _____ *kingdom and* _____ *righteousness, believing that the material things I need will be* _____ *. I choose for my* _____ *and* _____ _____ *to be free from the* _____ *of money,* _____ *,* _____ *and craving for earthly possessions. I am satisfied with my present circumstances and with what I have, being* _____ *, because You have promised You will not in any way fail me, nor leave me without support. I am* _____ *in Your* _____ *, that You will never leave me, nor forsake me, nor leave me helpless. I take* _____ *and am encouraged. I boldly say, that the Lord is my* _____ *, and I will not be seized with alarm. I will not* _____ *, or* _____ *or be terrified....*

I am assured that You will withhold no _____ _____ *from me as I walk* _____ *. The uncompromising are never* _____ *. I make it my ambition to live* _____ *and* _____ *, to mind my own affairs, to work with my hands so that I may bear myself* _____ *,* _____ *and*

_____, *and command the respect of the outside world, being self-supporting, dependent on no one, and having need of nothing.*

15. Prayer: Overcoming Bad Habits:

Father, I believe that my faith becomes effectual—divinely energized—by the acknowledging of every good thing which is in me, in Christ Jesus. Through my _____ *with Christ, I am a* _____ _____. *Old things are passed away and* _____ _____ *have become new.*

I was _____ *with Christ, nevertheless I live, yet not I, but Christ* _____ _____ _____. *I was buried with Him in* _____ *and raised together with Him by the* _____ *of the* _____ _____ *so that I might habitually live and behave in the newness of life. My old, unrenewed self was* _____ *to the* _____ *with Him in order that my body, which is the instrument of sin, might be made ineffective and inactive for evil and that I might no longer be a* _____ *of sin.*

Just as _____ *no longer has power over Jesus Christ, neither does* _____ *have dominion over me, through my union with Him. I consider myself dead to* _____ *and my relation to it broken. I am* _____ *only to God, living in unbroken* _____ *with Him, in Christ Jesus.*

16. A Prayer for Spiritual Growth:

Heavenly Father, I cease not to pray for _____, *that You may grant him/her a spirit of* _____ *and* _____ *and insight into the* _____ *and* _____—*in the deep and intimate* _____ *of You, having the eyes of his/her heart flooded with light so that he/she can know and understand the hope to which You have called him/her, and to know how rich Your glorious _____ is in the saints.*

I pray that _____ walks, lives and conducts himself/herself in a manner worthy of You, fully pleasing to You and desiring to please You in all things, bearing _____ in every good work and steadily growing and increasing in the knowledge of You....

I believe the good work You began in _____ will continue, right up to the time of Jesus' return, _____ it and _____ it to its _____ _____ in him/her, in Jesus' Name. Amen.

Discussion Question

Read Philippians 3:10-14. Identify the principles of the Apostle Paul's "determined purpose." How can you apply these principles to your own life and ministry?

_____

_____

_____

_____

_____

_____

_____

_____

_____

CONCLUSION

Brother Copeland has shared _____ and
_____ from God's Word that he has put to work
in his _____ life and _____. Any success he has enjoyed has been the result of a _____
_____ with Jesus and a _____ _____ _____.

*Heavenly Father, I approach Your throne _____
in the Name of Jesus... I can see from Your Word that I have
the _____ to expect my prayers to be answered—
not based on my _____, but based on my right-
standing in Christ Jesus. Your Word says if I draw near to
You, You will draw near to me. I desire a more personal
_____ with You and want to experience a rich and
_____ prayer _____.*

Prayer—Your Foundation for Success Answer Key

Introduction

1.   Effective Praying

2.   Jesus spent hours separated from the people, praying and fellowshiping with His heavenly Father

3.   Yes. Jesus said, "He that believeth on me, the works that I do shall he do also; and greater works than these shall he do; because I go unto my Father" (John 14:12). These greater works can be accomplished today, but only by believers who have a deep, sincere prayer life with God.

Chapter 1
Prayer Secrets

1.   The power of love, through prayer and intercession is the mortar which knits or holds the Body of Christ together.

2.   If a member of the Body of Christ is injured or weakened, the others are able to stand in prayer and make up for that weakness.

3.   Faith causes my prayers to bring results.

4.   Through the believer who is operating in faith.

5.   Fellowship is the "mother" of faith.

6.   My new birth into the family of God has given me the right to expect to get my prayers answered.

7.   The No. 1 priority in God's heart is to spend quality time with us daily.

8.   Bearing fruit is doing the works of Jesus, consequently pleasing the Father.

9.   The way to bear fruit is by prayer.

10.   Jesus stayed in tune with the Holy Spirit through fellowship and prayer with the Father.

11.   When you pray in faith and confidence, all of heaven's resources are at your disposal.

Discussion Question

Prayerfully consider which "prayer secrets" you learned from this chapter will apply to your life and ministry.

Chapter 2
Praying for Results

1.   The major cause of failure in Christian enterprises is a lack of prayer.

2.   Prayer is an attitude. It involves more than just making requests. It is communicating with God. You can live in an attitude of prayer every moment, being in constant communion and fellowship with your heavenly Father.

3.   In order to get results in prayer, you must be convinced that God wants to answer your prayers. In fact, He is as ready and willing to answer you as He was to answer Jesus during His earthly ministry.

4.   Prayer is communicating with God.

5.   The key to success in prayer is expecting results.

6.   The No. 1 rule in praying for results is to base your prayer on God's Word.

7.   God's Word is His will.

8.   Jesus said, "What things soever ye desire, when ye pray, believe that ye receive them, and ye shall have them." You must believe you receive when you pray.

9.   Romans 10:17 says faith comes by hearing, and hearing by the Word of God. Every believer is dealt the measure of faith (Romans 12:3). He must develop that faith by spending time in the Word of God.

10.   Jesus released power in His earthly ministry through words. Words carry power. The very forces of life and death are powered by the tongue (Proverbs 18:21).

11.   Acting on the Word puts faith into motion.

12.   Faith supported Peter on the water.

13.   (a) Do not concentrate on your circumstances; concentrate on the Word. What you see on the inside will determine your attitude. Use the spiritual weapons at your disposal. Second Corinthians 10:3-5 says, "For though we walk in the flesh, we do not war after the flesh: (For the weapons of our warfare are not carnal, but mighty through God to the pulling down of strong holds;) casting down imaginations, and every high thing that exalteth itself against the knowledge of God, and bringing into captivity every thought to the obedience of Christ."

(b) Maintain control of your mind.

(c) Refuse any thought or imagination contrary to your prayer.

(d) Refuse to give doubt any place.

(e) Be selective about the thoughts you entertain.

(f) Control your thought life according to Philippians 4:6-9. Learn to think on things that are true, honest, just, pure, lovely and of a good report.

14.   You can avoid failure by preparing to succeed.

15. When you pray in Jesus' Name according to the Word in faith, God will quickly respond to you (John 16:23).

Discussion Question

To get results, we must be convinced that God is ready and willing to answer our prayers, expect results when we pray in Jesus' Name and base our prayers on His Word. We must use the spiritual weapons at our disposal, maintain control of our minds and refuse any thought or imagination contrary to our prayers by casting down imaginations and bringing into captivity every thought to the obedience of Christ.

Chapter 3
The Battlefield of Prayer

1.   The Name of Jesus, the Word of God, the Holy Spirit, and the gifts of the Spirit. Our responsibility is to use them to fight the good fight of faith.

2.   If we're not keeping supplied by spending time in the Word and prayer, actively combating Satan, then he can easily overtake us.

3.   Your loins girt with the truth; the breastplate of righteousness in place; your feet shod with the preparation of the gospel of peace; the helmet of salvation; the sword of the Spirit; above ALL you are holding the shield of faith.

4.   When Satan tells you in your mind that you will never see the manifestation of your prayers, it is time to gird yourself with the truth. Ephesians 6:13-14 says, "...And having done all, to stand. Stand therefore, having your loins girt about with truth." In John 17:17 Jesus said, "Thy word is truth." Satan is a liar and the father of lies.

5.   In Mark 4, Jesus compares the Word of God to seed sown in the ground. When you plant seed, it produces a crop. So it is with the Word of God. When you plant the Word of God in your heart, it will grow and produce.

6.   When you pray in Jesus' Name, you immediately get the ear of God. The Name of Jesus carries ultimate authority in the spirit world. Satan knows the power invested in the Name, and he will retreat when it is spoken in faith.

7.   The power backing the Name of Jesus is the power of Almighty God!

8.   Effectiveness; confidence; Holy Spirit

9.   Helper; reality

10.   Authority; confident; authority

11.   Word; authority

12.   To redeem mankind, God had to destroy the union between man and the devil.

13.   Spiritually; physically

14.   He bore our disobedience and became its final sacrifice.

15.   Human race; total substitute; price; redemption

16.   Jesus

Discussion Question

We should use the spiritual weapons of the Name of Jesus, the Word of God, the Holy Spirit and the gifts of the Spirit.

Chapter 4
Prayer That Changes Things

1. (a)   The prayer of agreement

    (b)   Binding

    (c)   Loosing

    (d)   Petition and supplication

    (e)   Intercession

    (f)   United prayer

2. Things; God

3. That He is the same yesterday, today and forever (Hebrews 13:8).

4. Faith; the Word of God; circumstances

5. Success; well-being

6. Their prayers; Psalm 34:15

7. Every circumstance of life; Matthew 18:18-20

Verily I say unto you, Whatsoever ye shall bind on earth shall be bound in heaven: and whatsoever ye shall loose on earth shall be loosed in heaven. Again I say unto you, That if two of you shall agree on earth as touching any thing that they shall ask, it shall be done for them of my Father which is in heaven. For where two or three are gathered together in my name, there am I in the midst of them.

8. They agreed with the Word, read scriptures and prayed. They also wrote down their agreements as follows:

We hereby agree, according to Philippians 4:19 and Matthew 18:19 as follows: 'Father, we see in Your Word that You will supply all our needs according to Your riches in glory. We are setting ourselves in agreement that our financial need is met according to Your Word. We believe we receive (be specific)_____. We establish this agreement, in Jesus' Name. Amen.'

9. Two; agreement

10. Jesus said to forgive if you have aught against any.

11. Love; unforgiving heart; paralyzed

12. Agreement

13. Home; church; every other area; unselfish

14. Forgive; harmony; spiritual awareness; closeness; God

15. Harmony; agreement; deeper; personal fellowship; God

16. Police

17. Binding; loosing

18. Authority; Church; Satan

19.   Ultimate choice; receive

20.   Petition; supplication; request; higher power

21.   Power; united prayer

22.   Body; believers; one accord; Word; God; expect

Discussion Question

Prayerfully consider the type of prayer that would be most effective in your current situation. If you are using this workbook with a small group or Bible study, allow time for all to share.

Chapter 5
Intercessory Prayer

1. Intercession; behalf; others

2. His Spirit; manifestations; power

3. Privileged; blessed; witness; vessels; power

4. Because God does not do anything in the earth without the cooperation of a man.

5. Usher; coming; Church

6. Servant; God; child; God; servant; handmaiden; choice

7. You; serve; will; co-laborer

8. Love; dedication

9. Doorway; power

10. Intercession

11. Satan; blinded; minds; intercessory prayer; evil spirits

12. Love

13. Reconciliation; substitutionary; co-laborers

14. Restored; new birth; fellowship

15. Everything

16. Knowledge; love; love; others; soul-winners

17. Other tongues; valuable; intercessory

18. Separate yourself; world; alone with God

19. Intercession

20. One another

Discussion Question

Prayerfully consider how you can make time to intercede for a family member or friend this week.

Chapter 6
Kinds of Prayer

1. All prayer

2. Power

3. If; unbelief

4. Unbelief

5. Will; will; success

6. Peace; trusting Him

7. Thanksgiving; praise

8. Together; prayer; power

9. Words; power

10. Satan; faith; unbelief; power; God

11. Feel; worthy; praise; sacrifice

12. Priest; blood sacrifice; praise

13. Worry; stress; strain; death

14. Cares

15. Peace; Word; all; worry; anxiety; replace; the Word

16.   Operate; cast

Discussion Question

Prayerfully decide what kind of prayer would be most appropriate to address your need. If you are using this workbook with a small group or Bible study, discuss your answer with the group.

Chapter 7
Fasting and Prayer

1. Proclaimed; personal

2. Impress; fast; influence; impress; hungry; you

3. Situations; divine direction; proclaimed; believers; hearing from God

4. Proclaimed; minds

5. If you let others know you're fasting so you can receive admiration from them, their admiration will be your only reward. Fast in secret—just between you and your heavenly Father. Your reward will come from Him. He did not say, "If you fast," He said, "When you fast."

6. Admiration; men

7. Spiritual

8. Meditate; Word; observe to do; written; revealed; written; Word

9. Believer; love; Satan; destroying; love; profit

10. Spirit realm; inheritance; Fasting; spirit; healing; victory; strength; faith; power; spirit

11. Because of their unbelief. He had already given them power to cast out the devil (Luke 10:19). They had been allowing their flesh to rule them. They were not fasting,

praying and meditating on what Jesus had told them.

12. Pray; fast; minister; tapped into; power source; Holy Spirit; obedience; fasting; praying; Word; Lord; position; receive

13. Deliverance; correcting; anointing; anointing

14. Fasted

15. Jesus said if you will lose your life for His sake, you will find it.

16. (1) Decide the purpose of the fast.

(2) Proclaim the fast before the Lord.

(3) Believe you receive the reward, *before* the fast.

(4) Minister to the Lord.

(5) Minister to others.

17. Fasted; fruit; spirit; fruit; reborn human spirit; Holy Spirit; all; bear fruit; teach; bear fruit; teacher; intercessor; standby; helper; power; fruit

18. Love; joy; peace; longsuffering; gentleness; goodness; faith; meekness; temperance; spiritual forces

19. Body; spirit; dominate

Discussion Question

If you are using this workbook with a small group or Bible study, share how fasting has impacted your prayer life. Invite others to share their experiences.

Chapter 8
Hindrances to Prayer

1.   Answer; Word; His will; unwillingness; power; hindrances; overcome

2.   Bible; to; fro; earth; strong; hearts; perfect

3.   All; ask; believing; receive; few; now; then; all; ask; believing; *believing;* receive

4.   Doubt; unbelief; thief; blessings; separation; doubt; doubt; Word; His Word; His power; Doubt; God's Word

5.   Unbelief; His Word; Bible; chosen; see; feel; hinder

6.   Doubt; unbelief; final authority; religious tradition; deciding factor

7.   Pray

8.   Lack; knowledge; right-standing; Calvary; sin; righteousness

9.   Righteous; righteousness; righteousness

10.   Believes

11.   Faith

12.   Answer; pray, believing; right-standing; overcome

13.   Knowledge; right; void; power; Christian

14. Gloria and Brother Copeland were driving down the freeway one day. The car in front of them began to fishtail. The second time it came across the freeway, it hit the curb and started up on its side. Gloria shouted at the top of her voice, "Jesus, help them!" It was so strong when she shouted the Name of Jesus that the car slammed back down on all four wheels and straightened out, coming to a full stop. God responds to the Name of Jesus!

15. Forgive; vital; forgiveness

16. Strife; unforgiveness; Strife; unforgiveness

17. Strife; confusion; evil

18. Fellowshiping; prayer

19. Daddy; fellowship; Daddy; Father

20. Reveal; Spirit; faith; effective; fear; doubt; love; love; fear; fellowship; love

21. Word; fellowship; Spirit; fellowship; faith; expect

Discussion Question

Write about the hindrances to prayer you have encountered or share with your small group or Bible study. Open the discussion to include others' experiences and how each can be victorious in these areas.

Chapter 9
A Deeper Life in Prayer

1.   Prayer life

2.   Spirit man; mind; ears; voice; move; listening; intercessor; mouthpiece

3.   Accurate; sure; hoping

4.   Father; Jesus' Name; Name; free

5.   Pray

6.   Faith; heart

7.   Holy Spirit

8.   Reality; physical senses; spirit; soul; body; "earth suit"

9.   Faith

10.   Others

11.   Turmoil; others

12.   One another

13.   Intercessory prayer

14.   Spirit

15.   Unknown tongue

16. Other tongues; Spirit

17. Flesh; spirit; spirit; critical

18. Word; God

Discussion Question

Honestly evaluate where you are in your faith as you pray over situations and people in your life. If you are not fully persuaded God can fulfill His promises to you in these areas, write some of those promises, meditate on and confess them until faith comes and you are confident in the victory.

Chapter 10
Prayers

1. Speaking; confessing; power

2. God's Word; circumstances; prosper

3. Lord; Jesus

4. Sin; substitute; debt; credit

5. Holy Spirit; power; works

6. Holy Spirit

7. Faith; believing; men; truth

8. Void; Name of Jesus; infirmities; sicknesses; boldness; confidence; authority; redeemed; curse; tolerate

9. Love; hearts; love; gentle; compassionate; courteous; tenderhearted; humble-minded; peace; quietness; assurance; love; peace

10. True; heart; mouth; prevails; offspring; descendants

11. Government; authority; authority; rests; blessing; people; Lord; country

12. Covenant; mind; perfect; anxiety; circumstance; thanksgiving; light; salvation; dread; refuge; stronghold; peace

13. Temple; Holy Spirit; presence; leading me; guiding

me; steps; commit; trust; heart; understanding; day; night; mouth; Spirit; Word; quick; hearer; doer; blessed

14. Your; Your; supplied; character; moral disposition; love; greed; lust; confident; confident; faithfulness; comfort; helper; fear; dread; good thing; uprightly; forsaken; quietly; peacefully; becomingly; correctly; honorably

15. Union; new creature; all things; crucified; lives in me; baptism; power; Holy Spirit; nailed; Cross; slave; death; sin; sin; alive; fellowship

16. Wisdom; revelation; mysteries; secrets; knowledge; inheritance; fruit; perfecting; bringing; full completion

Discussion Question

Prayerfully consider how you can apply the principles of the Apostle Paul's determined purpose to your life and ministry and the changes that would result from their application. If you are using this workbook with a small group or Bible study, share your answers with the group and allow time for others to share.

Conclusion

Principles; precepts; personal; ministry; personal; relationship; rich; prayer; life; boldly; right; worthiness; relationship; successful; life

Prayer for Salvation and Baptism in the Holy Spirit

Heavenly Father, I come to You in the Name of Jesus. Your Word says, "Whosoever shall call on the name of the Lord shall be saved" (Acts 2:21). I am calling on You. I pray and ask Jesus to come into my heart and be Lord over my life according to Romans 10:9-10: "If thou shalt confess with thy mouth the Lord Jesus, and shalt believe in thine heart that God hath raised him from the dead, thou shalt be saved. For with the heart man believeth unto righteousness; and with the mouth confession is made unto salvation." I do that now. I confess that Jesus is Lord, and I believe in my heart that God raised Him from the dead. I repent of sin. I renounce it. I renounce the devil and everything he stands for. Jesus is my Lord.

I am now reborn! I am a Christian—a child of Almighty God! I am saved! You also said in Your Word, "If ye then, being evil, know how to give good gifts unto your children: HOW MUCH MORE shall your heavenly Father give the Holy Spirit to them that ask him?" (Luke 11:13). I'm also asking You to fill me with the Holy Spirit. Holy Spirit, rise up within me as I praise God. I fully expect to speak with other tongues as You give me the utterance (Acts 2:4). In Jesus' Name. Amen!

Begin to praise God for filling you with the Holy Spirit. Speak those words and syllables you receive—not in your own language, but the language given to you by the Holy Spirit. You have to use your own voice. God will not force you to speak. Don't be concerned with how it sounds. It is a heavenly language!

Continue with the blessing God has given you and pray in the spirit every day.

You are a born-again, Spirit-filled believer. You'll never be the same!

Find a good church that boldly preaches God's Word and obeys it. Become part of a church family who will love and care for you as you love and care for them.

We need to be connected to each other. It increases our strength in God. It's God's plan for us.

Make it a habit to watch the Believer's Voice of Victory Network and become a doer of the Word, who is blessed in his doing (James 1:22-25).

About the Author

Kenneth Copeland is co-founder and president of Kenneth Copeland Ministries in Fort Worth, Texas, and best-selling author of books that include *Honor—Walking in Honesty, Truth and Integrity*, and *THE BLESSING of The LORD Makes Rich and He Adds No Sorrow With It*.

Since 1967, Kenneth has been a minister of the gospel of Christ and teacher of God's Word. He is also the artist on award-winning albums such as his Grammy-nominated *Only the Redeemed, In His Presence, He Is Jehovah, Just a Closer Walk* and *Big Band Gospel*. He also co-stars as the character Wichita Slim in the children's adventure videos *The Gunslinger, Covenant Rider* and the movie *The Treasure of Eagle Mountain*, and as Daniel Lyon in the Commander Kellie and the Superkids™ videos *Armor of Light* and *Judgment: The Trial of Commander Kellie*. Kenneth also co-stars as a Hispanic godfather in the 2009 and 2016 movies *The Rally* and *The Rally 2: Breaking the Curse*.

With the help of offices and staff in the United States, Canada, England, Australia, South Africa and Ukraine, Kenneth is fulfilling his vision to boldly preach the uncompromised WORD of God from the top of this world, to the bottom, and all the way around. His ministry reaches millions of people worldwide through daily and Sunday TV broadcasts, magazines, teaching audios and videos, conventions and campaigns, and the World Wide Web.

Learn more about Kenneth Copeland Ministries
by visiting our website at **kcm.org**

We're Here for You!®

Your growth in God's WORD and victory in Jesus are at the very center of our hearts. In every way God has equipped us, we will help you deal with the issues facing you, so you can be the **victorious overcomer** He has planned for you to be.

The mission of Kenneth Copeland Ministries is about all of us growing and going together. Our prayer is that you will take full advantage of all The LORD has given us to share with you.

Wherever you are in the world, you can watch the *Believer's Voice of Victory* broadcast on television (check your local listings), the Internet at kcm.org or on our digital Roku channel.

Our website, **kcm.org,** gives you access to every resource we've developed for your victory. And, you can find contact information for our international offices in Africa, Australia, Canada, Europe, Ukraine and our headquarters in the United States.

Each office is staffed with devoted men and women, ready to serve and pray with you. You can contact the worldwide office nearest you for assistance, and you can call us for prayer at our U.S. number, 1-817-852-6000, seven days a week!

We encourage you to connect with us often and let us be part of your everyday walk of faith!

Jesus Is LORD!

Kenneth & Gloria Copeland

Kenneth and Gloria Copeland

CPSIA information can be obtained
at www.ICGtesting.com
Printed in the USA
FFHW020203110819
54137987-59827FF